Smart Storytelling

The Craft of Public Speaking

Deon Newbronner

This book is dedicated to everyone who

I have had the pleasure of meeting and

working with the past 25 years. You have changed me.

And I hope those who use this book will be changed too.

Table of Contents

Where did this book come from?

Growing up as the son of a preacher man, I've inherited something of a need to share stories. I witnessed storytelling daily, through my father and mother. They worked tirelessly for local communities, sharing stories and helping people. I seemed to follow suit.

I remember being the child in class who my classmates came to for help. But there was something else. I had an ability to see in others what they couldn't see in themselves. I was able to draw out of others the essence of them. Their story.

Up until recently my journey in business had been about creating a community for business folk to work in and be empowered by. This community approach disempowered me. I became everything to everyone and nothing to myself. The businesses failed because I didn't know my story and what it meant for who I am. I knew it. I just didn't know how to use it to live now.

I didn't know how best to share it. That's changed. I live it. I am it every day. I see it in the conversations I have with my son, William. I see it in the relationships I have with loved ones and friends. I am it when I am on the tennis court mastering my Federer backhand. I see it in the goals I set for myself. I now genuinely live by the poem I found at age fourteen for an art project:

Believe in yourself and in your plan (story)
Say not I cannot, but I can.
The prizes of life we fail to win,
Because we doubt the power within.

How to use this book?

This book is a practical guide to smart storytelling, the craft of public speaking. It will help you discover your story, speak with purpose, and have an impact. The key is to be open to trying new things. Practice makes perfect. This book is about application. It's about trying out the techniques and doing the exercises regularly and then taking time to reflect on your success.

Using the techniques and exercises regularly will help you cultivate a greater sense of self-belief when speaking. It'll also help you tap into your real potential and harness your inner power to build trust amongst the people you come into contact with.

You might want to scan over the book to get a bird's eye perspective. Then dive into bits depending on what you need right now. Perhaps you've got a talk coming up in a couple of weeks or days. You'd better get cracking if it's a couple of days.

Perhaps you need to get some specific guidance on how to incorporate your stories in your talk. Or you might want to work through the book methodically from start to finish. Do that. The book has been written so each of the Steps is progressive. They feed off each other, and they can stand alone too.

To get the very most out of this book there is one key ingredient. You have to make a time commitment of about three to four hours per week over at least eight to twelve months. This commitment to using the tools can yield tremendous results within a short space of time. Remember this book can be taken as a practical guide to developing some skills. Or it can be used far more effectively, as a life-changing tool that develops more useful habits and helps you communicate with power, passion and authenticity. It's up to you. It's changed my life and I guarantee you the tools have changed the lives of thousands of others too.

Does it take 21 days to form a habit?

No. It takes more. There are things you've got to do regularly. Think of this habit-forming process like a speaker, which you are. You may have felt downhearted knowing you've practiced your presentation or talk, and time and time again it doesn't seem to go well? Your nerves just seem to get the better of you. The audience doesn't really understand your point. You stumble over some words. You miss out bits of your talk. You know you could be better. It's just not happening. Sound familiar?

It takes time to form new habits

There was a plastic surgeon working in the 1950s. When he operated, like a nose job, he found that it would take his patient a minimum of 21 days to get used to seeing their new face. Or when a patient had an amputation, he noticed that the patient would sense a phantom limb for a minimum of 21 days before adjusting to the new situation.

Do you know where this story is going? Fast-forward a few decades and this 21-day habit-forming phenomenon has become ingrained in our collective brain. People forget that he said a minimum of about 21 days and shortened it to *it takes 21 days to form a new habit.*

So that's how society started to accept the common myth that it takes 21 days to form a new habit (or 30 days... or some other magic number). It's remarkable how often these timelines are quoted as statistical facts. It makes sense why the 21 Days myth took hold. It's easy to understand.

The time frame is short enough to seem achievable but long enough to be believable. Who wouldn't like the idea of changing your life in just three weeks?

Remember, Rome wasn't built in a day

So what's the real answer? How long does it take to form a new habit? And is there any science to back this up? It takes more than two months before a new behaviour starts to feel normal. How long it takes a new habit to form can vary widely depending on the individual behaviour, the person, and the circumstances. The truth is that it'll probably take you anywhere from two to eight months to begin to form new memories about your smart storytelling – doing it in different circumstances and living it.

What happens when we do take time to form new habits?

When you spend time reflecting on your past and present story, starting to explore the things that are important to you, you begin to notice the experiences you've had that have shaped you. Those experiences are real stories. Some powerful, some less so. They are your story. Within these incredible stories, you will find wonderful nuggets. Gems of delight. I call these your core messages, which when used in the right way in a talk or presentation can have a lasting impact on your audience.

There is no silver bullet here. You will find some of the tools I've included may be tricky or even strange. Rest assured they all work. They have been used by thousands of individuals for over twenty years. There will be frustrations and rewards. I aim to provide you with a map to guide you along a trail of self-discovery, with steps for you to get a foothold and begin to climb into smart storytelling and impactful speaking.

Many of us travel through life not ever realising who we truly are. We spend so much of our lives seeking external affirmation and being needy. I know I've been there. When I notice I'm living on autopilot I return to these tools and work through them.

A lot of us recognise our current story, but don't live it. Very few of us use our stories to connect with others. Whether in a public forum to ignite change and drive community or business success or in a more personal context at home with family. Be kind to yourself. Be patient and give yourself permission to try and fail. In the immortal words of the great man and great speaker Sir Winston Churchill, 'success consists of going from failure to failure without loss of enthusiasm.'

There is a science to storytelling

When I have lived in the now, and not worried about the future I am happy we've all experienced the power of *present-momentness*. Growing up I used to say, I can't wait till I'm 18 or some other age I thought had some significance. I think it was mainly due to my wanting to be accountable for my own decisions. Dad used to say to me, enjoy your school years Deon never wish them away.

It was his way of saying live now. Be present. Smart storytelling requires us to be present. When we do it has the power to engage, influence, teach and inspire listeners. That's why I argue for organisations to build a storytelling culture and place storytelling at the heart of their learning programmes. There's an art to telling a good story and we all know a good story when we hear one. But there's also a science behind the art of storytelling. Here's how it works starting with the science of the non-story.

We've all listened to and suffered through long PowerPoint presentations made up of bullet point after bullet point. Some may be meaningful to the presenter but lack the same sort of punch for the audience. Even if the presenter is animated when we hear the information being ticked off like this, the language processing parts in our brain known as the Broca's area gets to work translating those bullet points into the story from where we can find our own meaning.

The problem with this, however, is the story we come up with in our own mind may not be the same one the speaker is intending to convey through the data.

When a speaker delivers those same facts within a story, however, something else happens in the brain. Research suggests that when we hear a story not only are the language processing parts in our brain activated but all areas in our brain light up. Just like when we experience events. We live the storyteller's story for ourselves.

Storytelling engages the listeners' sensory cortex leading to a more connected and rich experience of the message. In short, the more a speaker conveys information in story form, the closer the listeners' experience and understanding will be to what the speaker is intending.

We know from experience that when we're listening to a good story, rich in detail, full of metaphor, and expressive of character, we tend to imagine ourselves in that same situation. Just think about all those scary stories told around the campfire as a child. Your heart rate increases, you get goosebumps, and the hair on the back of your neck stands on end.

Smart storytelling in a business setting might not be quite so dramatic or hair-raising, but can be more impactful than data alone.

Smart storytelling allows us to:

- Stimulate intense experiences without having to live through them.
- Experience the world before we have to experience it.

There are additional scientific elements at play.

Scientists are discovering that chemicals like cortisol and dopamine and oxytocin are released in the brain when we are telling a story. Why does that matter?

If we're trying to make a point stick, cortisol assists with formulating memories. Dopamine helps us regulate our emotional responses and keeps us engaged.

When it comes to creating deeper connections with others, Oxytocin is associated with empathy, an important element in building deeper or maintaining good relationships. So in real terms, you end your storytelling, talk, presentation, or meeting with a presence and an impact.

I like to think of storytelling as turning up a light on a dimmer switch. The more you use stories in your communications, the better the light, the brighter the light.

Perhaps most importantly, smart storytelling is central to meaning and purpose. It is through story that our minds form, and we examine our values and beliefs, as well as discern how they correlate with the values and beliefs of others. Listening to stories, we gain new perspectives and a better understanding of the world around us. We challenge and expand our understanding by exploring how others see and understand the world through their lens by sharing and listening to each other stories.

Ultimately, smart storytelling is about the exchange of ideas. About growth. And that's learning. That's why we must embed storytelling into our lives and our businesses.

If you're trying to engage, influence, teach, or inspire others you should be telling or listening to a story and encouraging others to tell a story with you.

You'll have plenty of science to back you up.

Notes and ideas:

The Smart Storytelling Model

Smart storytelling starts with you. It is you connecting authentically with the thoughts and feelings of others to motivate and inspire towards a common goal. You will do this, enhancing your trustworthiness when you:

1. Discover your Story – your past story and its value for you now, and your current story today. Using them (without attachment) will give you the freedom to create deep, emotion-fueled, and trusting connections with your audience.

2. Speak with Purpose – as this is the pathway to exceptional speaker performance and greater wellbeing.

3. Have an Impact – by planting the seeds that grow consistency and expectations, which become the funnel for future exceptional performance.

This model frames all the exercises and techniques in this book. If you practice the exercises and techniques, then over time you'll master each of the core elements of the Smart Storytelling Model.

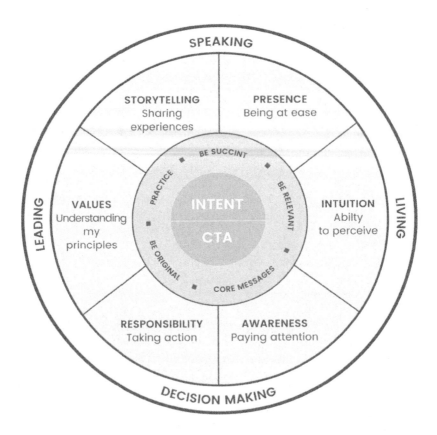

Notes and ideas:

Step One - What is your story and what is important to you now?

The River of Life

Purpose:

1. To understand your story.

2. To build a collection of your stories to connect, engage, motivate and influence others.

3. To reflect on your life experiences and discover moments when your experiences have influenced the things that are important to you.

Practice:

Your stories are found in everyday life experiences.

Go back over your river of life regularly. Reflect on your life experiences. Find the stories in your life that resonate. Stories don't have to be epic, they can be simple everyday stories. Use them to connect with who you are, and influence others.

Using these stories when speaking will have meaning for you. You will have the impact you desire, and authenticity no one can question.

Exercise:

Find a quiet space to work where you won't be interrupted for at least 2 hours.

Get a large sheet of paper and some coloured markers. You can spread out on the floor or tape your paper to the wall.

Before you begin, take a moment to relax, breathe, and be present. Imagine that you are on retreat and have all the time in the world.

Draw a river on the piece of paper winding from the lower left corner to the upper right corner. Label the lower left 'Birth and the upper right 'The Present.' Get creative! Break the rules! When you draw your river let its shape and features represent what's special about your life. I've seen swamps, bridges, waterfalls, forked rivers, and circular rivers. Don't strive for artistic perfection. Improvise and surprise yourself.

Now cast your mind back over your life.

Draw islands in the river, each representing places you've lived, key people you've known or who've influenced you, and any other 'landmarks' along the river of your life.

Have fun with this. Use different colours and symbols.

Along each side of the river, add tributaries representing challenging and affirming moments from your life. Think of those events, decisions, choices, and turning points that taught you something that made a lasting impact on who you are.

You could draw affirming tributaries in green on the left side of the river, and challenging ones in red on the right side. Write a keyword or symbol to remind you what each one represents.

Take a few minutes to look back over your river, adding any missing details. Make sure the river captures every aspect of your life: family, work, spirituality, and other life pursuits.

Once you've got this far, explore your river further:

1. Note your insights.

2. What patterns or trends do you notice?

3. What experiences and people were especially significant?

4. What are the stories of your experiences? Bullet-point your thoughts on your river or in a notebook about:

   - What happened?

   - Why do you think or feel it happened this way?

   - What is the message in this story? What's the nugget of the experience?

   - Why is this message important? What does it mean for you and/or others?

5. What are the core messages in each experience/story? Note these down in your notebook.

6. How could you relate these stories to how your values have formed over time?

7. What stories could you use in our talks or presentations? Remember: you do not need to use "the whole" story. You could use elements of the stories from your River of Life.

Here's some advanced river work...

Attach another piece of paper above the first and extend your river into the future. What do you envision happening, in your own life, your family, your business? What key choices or decisions lie ahead? Where would you like to be in five or ten years? How can you use these stories in your talks and presentations?

Keep this river with you when constructing your next talk or presentation (take a photo of it on your phone). Use these stories to pepper the way you engage with others, whether in a formal presentation sense or in a meeting or simple 1-2-1 conversation with someone.

Reflection Questions/Points:

1. What have some of your life stories taught you?

2. Find moments to share some of these stories with people, not just in a talk or presentation. Just in everyday life – at dinner or in the pub with friends.

3. Notice how the story makes you feel when telling it. Notice people's reactions to you and your stories. This can provide valued insight into choosing the stories to use and which parts of the story may not be necessary

Notes and ideas:

Step Two - How to become a Smart Storyteller?

Take a look at the Smart Storytelling Model on page 6. I want to draw your attention to each of the main core elements of the model. Smart storytelling takes time and practice. It's about approaching public speaking scenarios, whether in a 1-2-1, meeting or formal talk or presentation, with purpose. I call this your **intent**. Your intent for you, and your intent for your audience (their **call-to-action**). Allowing your intent to drive everything you say and do will ensure you are a Smart Storyteller, *speaking from the essence of you.*

By developing your **intuition** – your natural ability to perceive, sense, feel and know what is right for you, and what you are experiencing coupled with your **awareness** – your ability to pay attention, you will have the impact you desire. You will be able to engage others when speaking at a deeper and richer level.

To achieve this, you must take responsibility for the choices you make by **taking action** to cultivate a sense of **presence**, a state of being at ease. A sense of freedom and open-minded curiosity. And a willingness to discover the possibilities and trust the influential capability in your **story**. Here is how…

Notes and ideas:

The Power of Intent

Purpose:

To understand the impact a memorable and motivational intent can have on any public speaking or communication scenario.

Practice:

Use the passage below to practice this technique of owning your intent, and never forgetting it whilst speaking. This is a playful exercise. It has huge value when considering its application to your storytelling scenarios.

Think of your intent for speaking like a purpose or mission for a business. If it were your business, you're clear about its mission and purpose. You know what it is and how you are going to achieve it. Your business mission makes you and others in your business behave in certain ways. It makes you think in a certain fashion. Your business mission and purpose influence how you show up, to help you drive the business. The same principle applies to your intent for your storytelling, a talk, presentation, board meeting, 1-2-1, new business pitch... any situation where you are required to speak.

Simply put; intention is an attitude you adopt. It's a state of mind.

Exercise:

Find a place where you can read this tongue twister out loud. Go ahead, it will be fun.

Mr. Chops the butcher Shuts his shop–shutter,
Or perhaps his assistant Shuts his shop-shutter.
The butcher's shop–shutter Is a short shop–shutter.
And the butcher's short shop–shutter Should shut sharply.

Now read it again with the intent to read it to a group of four-year-old children. Imagine they're in front of you. Focus purely on reading it to these children. Be sure to remember how best to read to a group of small children. Focus on what is important to YOU when reading to four-year-old children.

What did you notice was different from the first time you read the passage out loud?

Your intent is clarified by answering the following question: How do I want to show up?

How you decided to show up – your intent (consciously or unconsciously) drove the changes in pace, vocal variety, and energy. The way you spoke, stood, behaved, and even acted was driven by your intent. Intent has the power to alter what people understand from you. Intent will help you connect with and engage an audience.

A further exercise to try is to find a poem you like. Then choose an intent. Forget about the potential audience for now.

See how the poem changes from intent to intent. For example, you could choose to be clear and precise. Then choose to be playful. Then review the differences between the two versions. Neither version is wrong. They're just different. You're different each time. It's still the real you, just speaking and performing differently.

The success of intent is driven by what I call the 3ms – *memorable, motivation, and mine*. With an intent constituted by the 3ms you will always be sure of your mission when speaking, and certainly, be the one people remember.

In other words, your intent should be no more than three words that you never forget (**memorable**) when speaking. They form your anchor for how you want to show up and be. They drive your attitude. The three words must **motivate** you to be a certain way – be a version of yourself, and you must identify your intent yourself (**mine**). It shouldn't be suggested to you by someone else. Otherwise, you'll end up play-acting.

See Circles of Intent diagram on page 17, for an example of intent and what the potential impact may be. I am asking you to consider and identify the first column on this diagram. The second column of circles on the left are examples of behaviours that may result from the intents I choose. Equally, on the right of the dividing line, an audience may react to my behaviours in certain ways – the first column on the right. And therefore, have a certain takeaway (far right column) or call-to-action from the experience of my talk/presentation.

When it comes to intent, I am not asking you to work *all* this out. I am using the diagram to illustrate *the possibilities* of what might be. What I am asking you to do is work out for yourself: far left column – intent, and far right column – Call-to-Action.

Reflection Questions/Points:

1. What did you notice was different in your vocal tone and pace when you delivered the tongue twister?

2. When storytelling, have a clear intent that is memorable, motivational, and mine. What was the impact of using the 3ms? Use feed-forward to review your success in using the power of intent.

3. Where might you use some of this newfound awareness of the power of intent to your advantage when speaking?

4. Ask yourself these questions after every talk, presentation, or speaking scenario, and use feed-forward to guide your responses.

Remember to Feed-Forward:

Ask yourself…

1. What did I do well that I should do more of?

2. What could I do to improve next time?

3. What am I grateful for in myself?

Notes and ideas:

Circles of Intent Diagram

My Audience

Result/Behaviour — **Take-home/C-T-A**

Think and reflect
Feel something

New Memories
Formed
Ideas
Eager

Listen intently
Ask questions

Deeper
understanding
Knowledge

Laugh and
enjoy

Enjoyment
Good experience
Content feeling

Me

**Intent (My 'why')
How do I want to show up?** — **My 'showing up'/
behaviour**

Thought-
Provoking

Challenge
Thinking
Ask Incisive
Questions

Clear-Concise

Articulate
Vocal Variety
Word Selection

Playful

Camp
Gesticulation
Pause and
breathe

Dimensions of Intent

Purpose:

To provide you with an in-depth understanding and practical application of the dimensions of intent.

Practice:

Use the following exercise when you next prepare a talk, presentation, or have a meeting to attend. Use this exercise to explore how a variety of different but complementary intents can be used to drive how you'll be in any communication scenario.

Exercise:

Identify your overall intent for yourself.

List out all your core messages and any stories you will use.

Now consider what your intent might be for each of your core messages and/or stories. Consider how these might connect/link with your overall intent of the talk/presentation/meeting. These sub-intents need to complement your overall intent for your talk or presentation.

Now play around with constructing your call-to-action. In other words, what do you want your audience to think, feel or do because of you showing up in the way that you have? Be sure you don't get caught up focusing purely on this. In other words, hold true to who you are and what you're planning to say, and crucially why you are saying it.

See the spider diagram in **Preparing your talks - being the one they remember** for a visual of what I mean.

Now practice out loud. Rehearse. Notice whether the varying intents help the content and drive your core messages and stories. Be sure they knit your entire talk/presentation together. Do they feed off each other? Is there a coherent path (for you) as you speak?

This is advanced stuff. If it doesn't come out right at first, try some alternative intents. Eventually, you will discover the most useful ones to use as your anchors and drivers for speaking.

I like to use my values as my intents. Then I know I am being authentic. From your River of Life, make a list of your most important values. Essentially, ask yourself: **what is important to me?** These are your standards of behaviour. Sometimes we are unconscious of some of our values.

Then, if you can identify a word that represents/sums up each value. Where relevant use your values-words-list as your intents when speaking. Notice how your intents drive how you show up.

Notes and ideas:

Emotive/Emotion-driven Intent

Purpose:

To understand how to use emotion to drive your talk and how you communicate.

Practice:

Cultivate a sense of mindfulness. Notice your emotions. Practice the skill of using your emotions to drive your connections with others. Remember you are not your emotions.

Exercise:

Undertake the *Dimensions of Intent* exercise. Now consider what emotion/s you want to convey for your talk to drive your core messages and stories.

Perhaps each story or core message needs its own emotion-driven intent.

Reflection Questions/Points:

1. Understanding intent and Call-to-Action are two sides of the same coin. They feed off each other. They must complement each other.

2. Remember to NOT just focus on your Call-to-Action. If you do your talk or presentation will never feel real to you and you may come across as presenting-by-numbers, patronising, or come across as just doing *the hard sell*. (Unless the hard *sell* is your intent.)

3. When doing a talk, presentation, or leading a meeting have a clear intent that is memorable, motivational, and mine. What was the impact of using the 3ms? Use feed-forward to review your success in using an intent.

4. When using an intent to drive your talk what did you notice about yourself and your audience?

5. Use feed-forward to respond to these questions. Ask yourself the feed-forward questions after every talk or presentation.

Remember to Feed-Forward:

Ask yourself…

1. What did I do well that I should do more of?

2. What could I do to improve next time?

3. What am I grateful for in myself?

Notes and ideas:

Principles of purpose-driven speaking

Purpose:

To maximise your impact using your story

Practice:

Whenever you begin to prepare a talk or presentation, walk into a room, lead a meeting, deliver a pitch or talk to your team, build what you say and do around being ORIGINAL, RELEVANT, and SUCCINCT. Use these principles as a measure of success for all your speaking interactions.

Exercise:

Always ensure you are being:

1. **Original** - personal stories (from your River of Life) and/or everyday stories that fit with your intent.

2. **Relevant** - pay attention to the audience. Understand who the audience is. Note how they are responding to your stories. However, pay attention to not being led too much by your audiences' reactions.

3. **Succinct** this is simply about less is more. Don't overload your audience with too much information.

Give it a go. Always remember, practice out loud. Then you'll know which stories work best.

See diagram on page 24.

Reflection Questions/Points:

1. What did you notice when you practiced out loud?

2. What stories could you use from your river or those noted in your notebook?

3. How have you decided to end your talk/presentation? Do you have a strong enough Call-to-Action (CTA) for your audience?

Remember to Feed-Forward:

Ask yourself…

1. What did I do well that I should do more of?

2. What could I do to improve next time?

3. What am I grateful for in myself?

Notes and ideas:

Talk/Presentation Triangle – Principles of purpose-driven speaking

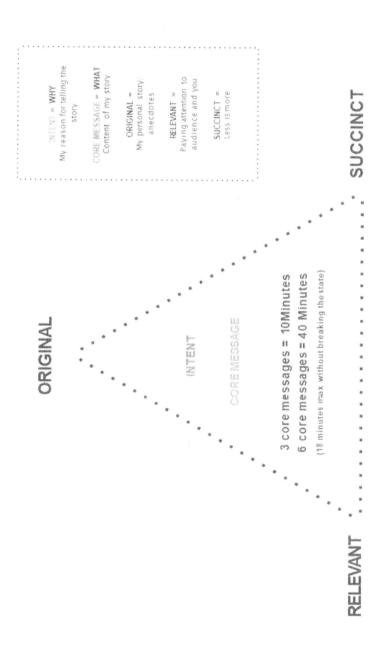

INTENT = **WHY**
My reason for telling the story

CORE MESSAGE = **WHAT**
Content of my story

ORIGINAL =
My personal story/
anecdotes

RELEVANT =
Paying attention to
audience and you

SUCCINCT =
Less is more

SUCCINCT

ORIGINAL

INTENT

CORE MESSAGE

3 core messages = 10Minutes
6 core messages = 40 Minutes
(18 minutes max without breaking the state)

RELEVANT

Preparing your talks - Being the one they remember

Purpose:

To use a simple method for preparing any speaking scenario.

Practice:

Being fully prepared for your talk/presentation/business meeting/1-2-1 is key to smart storytelling, and one of the best ways to speak with presence.

It'll also help to simply manage nerves and help your audience understand you better. It's the fundamental pillar for building confidence with smart storytelling.

Exercise:

As ever, start with identifying your intent. Get clear on the reason/s why you're speaking. This is not your brief. It is about identifying and adopting a specific attitude.

Identify your Call-to-Action. Remember this is about your audience. It should stem from your intent.

Use a spider diagram. In the centre write your intent. Circle it. Then write your Call-to-Action in the circle. Identifying what you will say is best tackled by identifying your core messages.

My rule of thumb is if you have 10 minutes of speaking time you ought to have no more than 3 core messages If you have 20 minutes of speaking time no more than 5 core messages and if you have 40 minutes of speaking time no more than 6 core messages.

Once you've identified your core messages list them on your sheet of paper around your circled intent. List them around the intent circle in a clockwise direction, forming the skeleton of your spider diagram. These are the 'titles' of your core messages.

When delivering your talk/presentation you might not have to say these out loud. But this may depend on whether you need to push home your core messages.

My rule of thumb is if your stories are strong enough then your core messages will come out loud and clear. Sometimes being very explicit about your core messages can make the audience feel you are preaching/telling them what to do. And they end up feeling patronised.

Then under each core message brainstorm a few stories from your experience that may help illustrate your core message.

Consider which storytelling techniques you wish to use.

Now practice your talk/presentation out loud. Yes, out loud. It's best reviewed having heard it out loud yourself.

Otherwise, you won't know how it sounds, and whether what you're saying fits with your intent and resonates with you. Or whether the storytelling techniques you've chosen are working. If it doesn't do all of these things it won't work for your audience either.

Remember you're not saying it out loud to memorise it. It's not a script.

Apply this process to each of the core elements/messages. Then knit it all together by saying the whole talk/presentation out loud.

If you need to create cue cards, then write them using the 'titles' of your core messages. Or if you need to use a slide show then remember to use one slide per core message, one slide for your introduction, and one for your conclusion. Remember, less is more. So don't crowd your slides with too much text.

Reflection Questions/Points:

1. Is your intent short memorable and motivational?
2. What did you notice when you practiced out loud?
3. What stories could you use from your notebook?
4. Did preparing with the use of a Spider-Diagram help? If not, could you approach your written prep differently? What way?
5. How many core messages are you wanting to convey?
6. How have you decided to end your talk/presentation? Do you have a strong enough Call-to-Action (CTA) for your audience?

Remember to Feed-Forward:

Ask yourself…

1. What did I do well that I should do more of?
2. What could I do to improve next time?
3. What am I grateful for in myself?

Notes and ideas:

Prep Spider Diagram

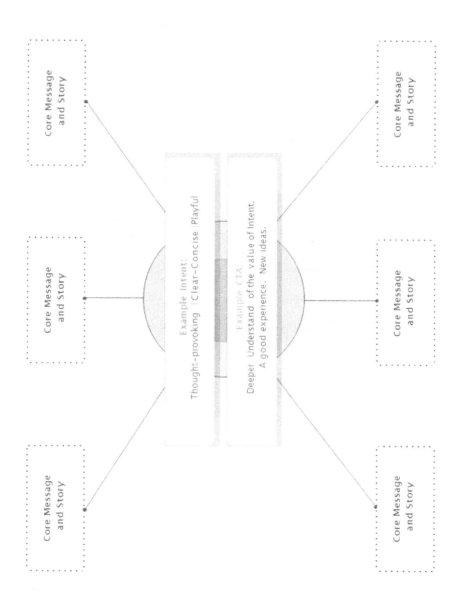

Let Your Body Do the Talking

The Holy Grail with all this speaking and leadership stuff is self-awareness and acting to improve your self-awareness. I define self-awareness as the ability to pay attention.

This next section is intended to help you become more aware of using your body to convey trust. This will free you up to use your body in better ways that serve your smart storytelling.

Purpose:

To improve your presence or address fears of using body and space.

Practice:

Body language is something powerful leaders know and use fluently. Try these approaches for better understanding and using your body congruently.

Exercise:

Become Aware. Next time you're in a public place, like a shopping centre or some large event, watch how people move. See if you can tell anything about their mood, physical condition, and personality by the way they walk and hold themselves.

When you meet a friend or loved one, and have a chance to see them move, try to gauge their frame of mind before they say a word.

Posture. People with presence tend to hold themselves erect. If you slouch and let your shoulders round in, it may communicate a lack of confidence. Correcting bad posture may take considerable effort. I often recommend Pilates training to strengthen your body to allow you to release your shoulders and help you stand up straighter. Tai chi, martial arts, Alexander Technique, or yoga can help too.

Facial Expression. Some people prefer a poker face, one that reveals nothing about their state of mind. While there are some situations when a poker face might be useful, in general, you'll connect with others better if you allow your · face to reveal what you feel. Not your nerves, but your feelings in the story you are telling.

Give mirroring a go. Just as you can mirror someone else's voice, you can mirror their facial expressions. Facial mirroring says, 'I understand you.' There's nothing more supportive for a public speaker than to look out at an audience and see facial expressions that say, *we're with you*.

Gesture. Notice how other people use their arms and hands when they talk. Some people, some entire cultures, favour great expression. Others prefer to be more self-contained. There are appropriate times for both approaches, but in general, you'll communicate better if you use congruent gestures (we address congruency in another module) with what you're saying. Again, notice what others do, including other professional speakers or television personalities you admire and pay attention to what you think works well.

Movement. This applies when you're standing and speaking to a group:

Use the Space. Walking, especially in combination with pausing, can be very powerful. Make an important point, then pause, and while pausing, move to a different position. Then begin speaking again. (It's usually not a good idea to talk while moving.) If you're telling a story, let the different locations on your 'stage' represent different locations in the story (like home and office) and move to those locations when the story changes scenes.

Distance. Moving can change the energy level in the room. If you stand far from the audience, or behind a podium, that's a safe, low-energy place for you to the audience. But if you move toward the audience, you create a more intimate connection.

And, if it's physically possible, moving right up to or into the audience will help pick up the energy level in the room enormously. Here's a wake-up call…whenever you enter someone else's space, an individual's or an audience's, you create a moment of high potential, even danger. Your audience will become more alert. Will you call on someone? What do you want? What are you going to do? People wake up when the speaker approaches. Be aware of that dynamic and use it to add energy and emphasis to your message.

Try these different techniques and use Feed-Forward to reflect on their appropriateness. Remember I'm not asking you to critique yourself.

Taking Up Space. Some people seem to take up more space in a room than their physical size.

These exercises will give increased confidence to your bearing:

* **Grounding.** Walk around in an empty room. Think of yourself as solidly grounded, with your centre of gravity not in your chest but in your pelvis where your legs and hips connect. Think of yourself as solidly connected to the earth.

* **Expanding.** Then, think of yourself as literally taking up more physical space than your body requires. Imagine you're much larger than you are. Walk through the room with your arms extended wide. Imagine you're a king or queen, someone of enormous authority because people usually give such figures a lot of space. Imagine you are in your own home, greeting and welcoming the people around you.

* **Owning**. Go into the room where you'll speak and make yourself comfortable with it beforehand. Don't be shy - this technique works! If you can't get into the room then visualise it.

* **Eye Contact**. I've saved one of the most important means of body language expression for last. Eye contact when you're expressing yourself is critical. Without maintaining eye contact you risk losing the attention of the listeners. It's just as important in a meeting or presentation as in a 1-2-1. In my experience, some speakers make two major errors.

    First, they want to include everyone and so their eyes shift much too rapidly around the room. Or even worse, they speak to the back of the room. Second, they focus too much on looking at the materials they're presenting, whether it's a speech in front of them or a slide projected on a screen. In both cases, they haven't used their eyes to connect with the audience.

So, look at the audience. Look individuals in the eye. The people around them will feel you are connecting with them too. Don't stare though. Don't focus on one person alone for your whole talk/presentation.

Reflection Questions/Points:

1. What have you noticed about the way you move and use your body?

2. What have you noticed about the way others use their body?

3. What messages do you pick up from other people's non-verbal signals? What relevance does this have for you and your speaking?

4. Where might you use some of this newfound awareness to your advantage when speaking?

Remember to Feed-Forward:

Ask yourself...

1. What did I do well that I should do more of?

2. What could I do to improve next time?

3. What am I grateful for in myself?

Notes and ideas:

Be in your body - belly-breathing

Purpose:

To deal with nerves and tension when speaking your truth, and to become more present.

Practice:

The goal of these exercises is to train the body to breathe with the belly automatically.

Exercise:

Sit comfortably or stand in a neutral position. I call this being *centred*. Starting from the top of your head, move your awareness slowly down through your body, noticing and releasing any tension.

Lay one hand on your belly and one hand on your chest, so you can notice where your breath is. When we sit or stand our habit is to breathe up in the chest. If you have trouble feeling the breath in the belly, imagine you're breathing through a straw. Try inhaling through your nose.

You can also experiment with filling your entire lung capacity, breathing into both the belly and the chest. Imagine your inhalation is like filling a glass with water, beginning from the bottom - the lowest part of the belly – and filling to the top – the top of the chest. Once you've taken this very big breath in, try letting it out on a big sigh of relief.

Finally, return to your regular breathing, just noticing the rise and fall of the belly with your breath.

Training Regime. The best way to become a natural belly-breather is to undertake a regular daily practice. Since it's easiest to locate belly breathing when lying down you can take two minutes before you go to sleep at night and when you wake up in the morning. Just place your hands on your belly and your chest and do the exercise above. After a couple of weeks, you'll notice yourself naturally breathing this way as you go about your day.

Reflection Questions/Points:

1. What impact have you seen when naturally belly-breathing?
2. When are you using belly-breathing?
3. How might you extend your practice into everyday life?
4. What has been the effect on your talks, presentations or meetings?

Notes and ideas:

Circles of Being

Purpose:

To explore how your energy (and state of mind) in the moment can affect your presence (your ability to connect).

Practice:

Notice your energy and thinking moment to moment and day to day. Notice how you can change your energy and move through each circle in any conversation.

Exercise:

When you speak there's a temptation to become wrapped up in what you're doing and saying. But your performance takes on a whole different level when you start noticing the effect you have on the world around you.

Circles of being is used to master your ability to connect authentically with the thoughts and feelings of your audience. It's a technique used to develop a state of *being* through which you can influence your audience. It's an energy that fuels a certain kind of performance and a way of being.

Next time you are preparing a talk or presentation play around with your energy.

Explore the effect you can have on an audience by altering your energy moment-to-moment. Circles of being can help you live your intent in each moment. It aids *being in the moment*. The three circles represent the following:

First Circle: Your focus is on yourself and it's intimate. Usually used in 1-2-1 conversations. Your voice is quiet, and your body is still and unaffected. It's almost as though you're speaking to yourself. It's very personal and it can be used to create a sense of curiosity. It's introspective and enticing. At its worst, you may be seen as hiding your presence away inside you. Too much first circle will diminish the perception of your presence, and you might look nervous or not confident.

Second Circle: You are fully present and you are in the moment. Your focus is placed outside yourself. You speak to affect other people. As a speaker and leader, you require presence. The second circle gives this and it's here you connect with people. In the second circle, you make a true connection because you know you're truly present and the audience feels connected to you.

However, it can be challenging to stay in second all the time, so be ok with moving into first and third circle as appropriate.

Third Circle: You possess what I call a 'generalised connection outward'. It can feel a little over the top. Gestures are big and expansive. The energy is high. However, when used in large spaces, being in Third Circle can have the right impact.

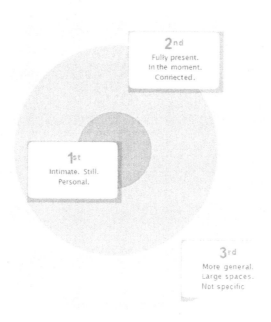

2nd
Fully present.
In the moment.
Connected.

1st
Intimate. Still.
Personal.

3rd
More general.
Large spaces.
Not specific

Reflection Questions/Points:

1. What have you noticed about the way you move and use your body when in different circles?

2. How has your voice changed in the different circles?

3. Have there been opportunities to try circles of being out unconsciously?

4. Do you have a preferred circle?

Remember to Feed-Forward:

Ask yourself...

1. What did I do well that I should do more of?

2. What could I do to improve next time?

3. What am I grateful for in myself?

Notes and ideas:

The 3 Ps of storytelling

Purpose:

To explore the craft of constructing a good story using purpose, people, and places.

Practice:

Build your stories using a framework that works for you, and review them as often as possible. Smart storytelling is all about honing your signature style.

Begin to reflect on the stories you've told. You can also use this framework to assess your stories to ensure they have the core elements of a great story.

These simple frameworks will help lead to rich and rewarding storytelling.

Exercise:

Stories are compelling. They are unique. Facts and knowledge can be disputed. Your stories are yours. They cannot be disputed.

Stories engage, connect, challenge, and move an audience to think, feel or do something.

When telling your stories, it's important to remember that the audience will interpret your stories in their way. This is why it is crucial you're clear and never forget your intent. The first core element of smart storytelling is intent. Remember intent is simply asking yourself, how do I want to show up? It's your motivation for standing up and talking.

First, the…

Purpose - why am I speaking? Be clear about this. Remember there are two dimensions.

The first is your motivation. Second, is your call to action for the audience. Figure out these two dimensions. And never forget them when you're presenting, doing a talk, or leading a meeting. Have them etched in your mind. They'll drive your talk or presentation and give it focus.

Then, the…

Place - what action happens and where does it take place? Describe, with as much detail as you can, the action of events. (The moment-to-moment happenings.) Then add in the locations. Even going as far as naming the locations as this anchors the story in a reality that is translatable.

Then finally…

People - who is there and what do they think and feel? This is all about the characters in your story and their emotional experience. This needs to be delivered with language that's appropriately emotive (appropriate to your intent and/or call-to-action).

This is when the audience connects with what you're saying in a manner that is personal to them. This element makes the difference between presenting by numbers and making a real impact. In other words, it's the difference between going through some automatic notion of presenting versus *talking with* an audience and connecting with them.

We make these emotionally driven connections because of the limbic part of the brain that drives our decision-making. The limbic brain deals with everything emotional, like our emotional responses to decisions. If we're clear about WHY we're speaking and if we understand our emotional motivation for speaking and we convey it implicitly in our talk or presentation, then the audience will connect with us. They might not remember how or what you have said, but they will remember how you made them feel. And that should be our aim when speaking in public and in your day-to-day business and personal life.

Reflection Questions/Points:

1. When you next prepare your talk or presentation practice some of your stories out loud.

2. Remember to always start with your intent and identify your call-to-action. (See the Power of Intent.)

3. Then feed-forward after your talk or presentation.

Remember to Feed-Forward:

Ask yourself…

1. What did I do well that I should do more of?

2. What could I do to improve next time?

3. What am I grateful for in myself?

Notes and ideas:

Colour and Advance

Purpose:

To understand the techniques of adding emotion and feeling, and marrying facts and information to create a powerful story.

Practice:

Pay attention to your use of emotional language and the facts you share when you're telling stories.

Exercise:

Next time you're out at a pub, restaurant or just talking to friends, start to notice the way you embellish the stories you share. Begin to make conscious choices about the use of emotion and facts in your storytelling. Notice how often you share information and facts.

Notice the frequency of statements such as:

Kathy left to go home. When she got home she unpacked her shopping. She put the kettle on. She put the shopping away. She sat down and had a cup of tea with a slice of cake.

And how often you may add phrases such as:

Kathy got home exhausted and feeling angry, and she began to unpack her shopping with gusto. She didn't want to spend the next hour doing it. She had other plans. Plans for a delicious slice of cake, which she'd just bought. And a hot cup of tea. She put the kettle on. It was her favourite thing to do...relaxing with a slice of Madeira cake and a cuppa. Just putting her feet up and letting go of all the frustrations of shopping just before Christmas.

Neither of the above versions of what Kathy did when she got home is wrong. Both have equal value in storytelling. A great deal will depend on your intent. You probably tell stories like the second version more often than you think. What you're doing, if you share stories in this way, is colouring and advancing. These are the two most important aspects of storytelling.

Colour adds emotion and feeling. It adds depth and meaning to your story.

Advance provides facts and information. It moves your story along.

Both are equally important. There isn't a hard and fast rule to when you should colour or when you should advance. Although the general rule of thumb is that you should mix it up. Sometimes you might advance for a while. Sometimes you might colour for a bit. In other moments you may do both at the same time. What you must do is ensure there's colouring and advancing in all your presentations and public speaking. Because people will connect to both.

Reflection Questions/Points:

1. When colouring and advancing in your storytelling what have you noticed happens to your audiences' responses?

2. Notice when you colour and advance when telling everyday stories at dinner or down the pub.

3. Make a point to colour if you generally present information, or if you notice you move presentations along quickly.

4. Where might you use some of this newfound awareness of colouring and advancing to your advantage when speaking?

5. Use feed-forward to reflect on your storytelling effectiveness.

Remember to Feed-Forward:

Ask yourself…

1. What did I do well that I should do more of?

2. What could I do to improve next time?

3. What am I grateful for in myself?

Notes and ideas:

Dialogue and Narration

Purpose:

To understand the technique of dialogue and narration to convey feeling and a deeper sensory experience.

Practice:

Combine dialogue with other storytelling techniques such as Colour and Advance, Anchoring, etc. And remember good story construction always has the 3 Ps.

Exercise:

When using dialogue be brave. You can create characters using physical movement or physical nuances, as well as different voices. If you do this remember to keep it simple and consistent.

You can also simply have a dialogue without the above. Remember everything is driven by your intent. It's driven by how you want to be.

You can simply replace an explanation of something with a conversation between two people. Dialogue is more powerful than narration, but both have their place. Dialogue puts the audience into the scene, allowing them to hear exactly what was said. Dialogue is also shorter and punchier.

With the change in vocal variety, dialogue can help you alter the pace, pitch, and volume of your voice to reflect the emotions of the different people in the scene.

Compare this dialogue…

And they watched for a few minutes, and he turned to his mother and said, "Mrs. Lynne, Gillian isn't sick; she's a dancer. Take her to a dance school."

With this narration…

And they watched for a few minutes and the doctor told Gillian's mother that her daughter wasn't sick.

She was a dancer and that she should be taken to dance school.

You can FEEL the difference.

Remember, when you use dialogue, don't explain what you're about to do. Just do it.

Reflection Questions/Points:

1. When using dialogue in your storytelling what have you noticed happens to your audiences' responses?

2. Notice when you use dialogue in everyday stories at dinner or down the pub.

3. Where might you use some of this newfound awareness to your advantage when speaking?

4. Use feed-forward to reflect on your storytelling effectiveness.

Remember to Feed-Forward:

Ask yourself…

1. What did I do well that I should do more of?

2. What could I do to improve next time?

3. What am I grateful for in myself?

Notes and ideas:

Being specific

Purpose:

To turn your story into a mental movie.

Practice:

When crafting your story, it's important to provide specific details, while still remembering less is more. Don't overload the story.

Exercise:

When constructing your talk use specific names, places, dates, sizes, colours, etc. to convey specifics about the characters, what took place, and where it was. Remember the 3 Ps.

For example, instead of saying, the man was tall, say, John was 6 foot 5 inches. Instead of saying, *I was speaking to a large group of people, say, I was speaking to 500 CEOs at 1 pm*.

The non-specific detail doesn't help the audience see the scene. Non-specific statements such as *the man was tall* don't help the people in your audience to picture the characters and the scene in their mind. Saying, *he was about 6 foot 5 inches, with ripped muscles* provides enough detail for the audience to be able to see the character and the scene, as well as adding credibility to your talk.

Remember don't explain what you're about to do. Just do it.

Reflection Questions/Points:

1. When being specific in your storytelling what have you noticed happens to your audiences' responses?

2. Notice when you're saying too much. Remember, less is more.

3. Where might you use some of this newfound awareness to your advantage when speaking?

4. Use feed-forward to reflect on your storytelling effectiveness.

Remember to Feed-Forward:

Ask yourself…

1. What did I do well that I should do more of?

2. What could I do to improve next time?

3. What am I grateful for in myself?

Notes and ideas:

Anchoring

Purpose:

To understand the technique of anchoring to hit home a core message.

Practice:

Combine anchoring with other storytelling techniques such as Colour and Advance, the 3 Ps, etc.

Exercise:

When using anchoring you must be very specific. An anchor is the primary takeaway that you want your audience to leave with.

An anchor is a single sentence or phrase repeated at least 3 times throughout your talk. You must start with the anchor, repeat it somewhere in the middle of the talk, and you must end with the anchor.

Your anchor must be punctuated by a pause before it, and then again after it before you continue with your story.

The same words in the same order must be used on all 3 occasions. As a variation, you may use a variety of different tones when saying your anchor. As with the anchor itself, the tone should be driven by your intent.

Each time the anchor is said it must be book-ended by a definitive pause. Remember, don't explain what you're about to do. Just do it.

Reflection Questions/Points:

1. When using an anchor in your storytelling what have you noticed happens to your audiences' responses?
2. Notice when you use anchoring in everyday stories at dinner or down the pub.
3. Use feed-forward to reflect on your storytelling effectiveness.

Remember to Feed-Forward:

Ask yourself…

1. What did I do well that I should do more of?
2. What could I do to improve next time?
3. What am I grateful for in myself?

Notes and ideas:

Using ALL the Senses

Purpose:

To understand the technique of using the five senses to help your audience experience the world you are creating.

Practice:

Provide a narrative description of the scene/s in your story by using most of or all these senses in your talks - visual, auditory, kinaesthetic, olfactory, and gustatory.

Exercise:

You can help your audience create a mental picture of your characters and stories by using all or most of the five senses.

The true power of this type of technique is that it provides the audience with a wealth of sensory information to make your story come alive. You can visualise what's happening like a motion picture inside your mind's eye.

Using all or most of the five senses in your talks includes:

Visual (sight) - What can you see in the story? This tells the audience about things and people who are there. Be very descriptive and detailed when describing the key items and people present in your story.

Auditory (sound) - What can you hear?

Kinaesthetic (touch, emotions) – What can you feel? (Both internally as an emotion, and also the physical sensations of touch.)

Olfactory (smell) – What can you smell?

Gustatory (taste) – What can you taste? This could be specific to flavours, or it might be inferred; as in leaving the audience with a bad taste in their mouths.

Blending the elements of the five senses helps to bring your story to life. Pay attention to how often or not you're aware of their use.

Your audience will internalise their experience of your story, making what you say more memorable.

Remember, less is more. You don't have to make your descriptions long and detailed. And removing any need to explain what you're doing will free up space to play with storytelling techniques.

Reflection Questions/Points:

1. When using the five senses in your storytelling what have you noticed happens to your audiences' responses?

2. Where might you use some of this newfound awareness to your advantage when speaking?

3. Use feed-forward to reflect on your storytelling effectiveness.

Remember to Feed-Forward:

Ask yourself...

1. What did I do well that I should do more of?

2. What could I do to improve next time?

3. What am I grateful for in myself?

Notes and ideas:

Villain, Victim and Hero

Purpose:

To understand the technique of using villain, victim and hero as metaphors to help your audience experience the world you're creating.

Practice:

Provide a narrative description of the scene/s in your story by using this triangle of villain, victim and hero.

Exercise:

You can help your audience create a mental picture of your core message by using characterization of the *villain*, the *victim* and the *hero*. Every good story has these three elements in it.

Think about Star Wars for a moment. It's <u>not</u> a story about intergalactic battles and Stormtroopers. It's a story about the hero (Luke Skywalker) overcoming the villain (Darth Vader) and rescuing the victim (Princess Leia). We are drawn in by Luke's purpose, his intent on saving her from Darth Vader. We are taken on a journey to interstellar locations with wonderfully strange and delightful characters. We get to know these people. What they think, and how they feel. We connect with these people. They have similar emotional responses and thoughts as we do. We buy into the story.

Have a go yourself…

Present yourself as the hero. But be sure to present yourself as the hero without ego, but driven by your personal values.

Let the thing that frustrates your audience be the villain e.g. bad communication. And your audience is the victim. You could be the hero. Spelling out to them how you'll save them from bad communication.

Remember, less is more. You don't have to make your descriptions long and detailed. And removing any need to explain what you're doing will free up space to play with storytelling techniques.

Reflection Questions/Points:

1. What did you notice happened to your audiences' responses?

2. Where might you use some of this newfound awareness to your advantage when speaking?

3. Use feed-forward to reflect on your storytelling effectiveness.

Remember to Feed-Forward:

Ask yourself...

1. What did I do well that I should do more of?
2. What could I do to improve next time?
3. What am I grateful for in myself?

Notes and ideas:

Story Spine

Purpose

To provide a model framework for a well-constructed story.

Practice:

Provide a narrative description of the scene/s in your story by using this story spine. And as many or as few "because of that…" elements as relevant.

Exercise:

The well-constructed story has a beginning that establishes a routine, an event that breaks the routine, a middle that shows the consequence of having broken the routine, and a climax that sets the resolution of the story in motion, and the resolution.

Here is an example of the tool you can use. However, you do not have to use these specific phrases:

- Once upon a time…
- Every day…
- But, one day…
- Because of that…
- Because of that…
- Because of that…
- Until finally…
- And, ever since then…

Reflection Questions/Points:

1. What did you notice happened to your audiences' responses?
2. Where might you use some of this newfound awareness to your advantage when speaking?
3. Use feed-forward to reflect on your storytelling effectiveness.

Remember to Feed-Forward:

Ask yourself…

1. What did I do well that I should do more of?
2. What could I do to improve next time?
3. What am I grateful for in myself?

Notes and ideas:

Step Three - How to live Smart Storytelling?

It takes courage to be the person you are and to live how you choose. There's no magic pill or solution to make this happen, especially in a world that constantly sends you messages about who you ought to be.

In my experience of helping 1000s of individuals over the past 25 years become smart storytellers, you must let go.

Let go of the old way of doing things. Those unhelpful habits.

Even though I've said you have to reflect on the past, because there you'll find your story, you also need to let it go. The difficulty in letting go is that the mind gets into ruts. And if you're anything like me – human – you'll overthink things or brood over stuff you've done or haven't done. Whether you shared that story well last week right. Whether your intent was strong enough, or even whether you paused enough. We then start to feel guilt and shame. And let's face it guilt and shame are all around us. Western society has been built on it. Guilty for feeling not good enough. Shame for not living up to our own expectations.

Using the techniques in this book to help you become a smart storyteller and speak with confidence will certainly help. I'm not suggesting that practicing these self-reflection techniques is going to take away all ills. But by using them regularly they will help you live your master the craft of public speaking.

Notes and ideas:

Always Feed-Forward, never Feedback

Purpose:

To understand the value of Feed-Forward in building confidence in presenting and public speaking.

Practice:

There are lots of quick fixes that can act as a sticking plaster to help make your presentations and public speaking better. But if you want to build a strong foundation, then you need to take stock. And appreciate yourself and those around you. Using Feed-Forward can help with this.

Exercise:

Feed-Forward is based on three clear steps. It's a mechanism that's all about focusing on the positives. When you give yourself feedback, or when you seek feedback from others, it can sometimes focus too much on the negatives. Looking back is not going to help you progress as a smart storyteller, public speaker, or presenter. Without wishing to sound too much like Lady Macbeth…what's done is done.

Feedback focuses on the past. Feed-Forward is all about your future…your future as a smart storyteller. Let's take a walk through the steps…

Step 1 - The first step is all about asking yourself, 'What did I do well?' You need to give yourself space to say 'Yes, that worked. Yes, I did it.' It might be along the lines of appreciating aspects of your last presentation or talk that went well for you. It could be how you altered the pace of your delivery or how you relied on fewer slides. Or how well your intent worked. It's important to be truthful.

Step 2 - Ask yourself about what you will do next time to change things and improve. But remember, it's not about what you did 'wrong.' This step focuses on potential solutions and improvements, not on past problems.

It's about questioning what you'll do the next time you deliver this talk, or a similar presentation, to improve. It could be thinking about the possibility of using a different personal story to get more of an audience reaction. Or deciding to spend more of your allotted time to hit home the parting shot of your talk.

Step 3 - Here comes the rub…this is when you need to ask yourself, 'What am I grateful for? What should I give thanks for?' It could be thinking about being grateful for feeling confident before you started. Even though it may have been the first time you were delivering some new material in your presentation.

Or it could be simply showing gratitude for the level of audience engagement you felt. It can be anything. Again, what's important here is being truthful. Don't just pay lip service to step 3. It's just as important as the other steps.

Sometimes the 3rd step can be quite tricky to get used to. But ultimately step 3 is about cultivating a sense of happiness with yourself. There's a lot of stuff out there on the internet about how to do this. Some of it can come across as a bit corny. But it has more than a bit of truth in it. It has a lot of truth in it. And let's face it, why wouldn't you want to create a sense of happiness with your storytelling, presenting, and public speaking?

Notes and ideas:

Rituals of self-reflection

Purpose:

To proactively create time to reflect on my truth, and whether I am living it.

Practice:

Instead of waiting for a crisis, self-knowing leaders regularly and systematically review their experience, distilling what there is to learn. In addition to the River of Life, use one or more of these approaches regularly:

Exercise:

Take Notes. Keep a journal of your thoughts and feelings, particularly for insights regarding your own behaviour, challenges you're facing, and how you see your path of growth and learning.

Retreat. Get away regularly. A change of physical perspective often prompts self-reflection, particularly in moments of quiet amidst the beauty of nature. Even a mindful stroll around a local pond or park can prompt deep insight.

Study Others. Reflecting on other people and what makes them respond to others (or what limits them) can enrich your examination of yourself and your own experience.

Clear the Mind. When the mind is still, like a clear pool, we can better see our reflection. Find a ritual that works for you. Yoga, tai chi, meditation, breathing and relaxation exercises, and physical exercises such as walking or jogging are all ways to calm and centre the mind for deeper self-reflection.

For guided meditation, I use the buddhify app every day. Download it onto your phone. You can even use it when travelling.

Notes and ideas:

Congruency

Purpose:

To become more aware of any insincerity, lack of credibility, or lack of trust.

Practice:

A great tool for noticing congruence versus incongruence is voicemail. By taking the body out of the equation, we can focus specifically on the quality of the voice, and how it matches or contradicts, the content of the message.

Exercise:

Become a connoisseur of incoming messages. Does the caller's delivery match the words?

TED has a lot of amazing speakers and some not-so-amazing speakers. Watch the YouTube videos and notice what works for you and what doesn't work for you.

Notice how other speakers use changes in pitch, volume, tempo, enunciation, and vocal quality to convey warmth, concern, humour, urgency, etc. How effective is it?

Listen to your outgoing message on your phone and critique it for congruence. Redo this as many times as necessary until it carries just the right tone you wish to convey.

Notes and ideas:

Flexibility - be open to unexpected outcomes "Yes and …"

Purpose:

To develop a more open-minded approach to speaking and living your truth.

Practice:

The fundamental skill of successful improvisation is being able to accept another's offer and then build on it. This requires listening, flexibility, and creativity. Try practicing *'Yes and...'* behaviour at work, when you're preparing your talks or when you're just at home and having a conversation with someone.

Exercise:

First, notice any existing tendency you may have to be attached to your ideas, to automatically critique others, or to give a simple thumbs up or down on what others are saying.

Then, see what happens if you try using 'Yes and …' behaviour. Consciously listen to their idea.

Let your first thought be: *What can I agree with here?* Try this with yourself too. Instead of seeking first to critique yourself, perhaps seek first to understand why you may have said what you did.

In your response, accept and acknowledge the idea, and then build on and extend it. Notice his/her reaction.

Try doing this in a variety of different conversations and notice what results you achieve

If 'yes and' is too challenging, then rather than falling into *yes* but try responding with yes how. This allows for offers to be accepted and ideas to be built upon.

Notes and ideas:

Change your perspective

Purpose:

To deal with self-judgment that inhibits you.

Practice:

Your inner critic consists of the voices inside your head that constantly evaluate you. It can be enormously useful to confront your inner critic and get these voices out in the open.

Exercise:

Write a letter from your inner critic to yourself that includes all the nasty, judgmental things it wants to say to you. Explore why and in what situations your inner critic thinks that you're not good enough or that you're a failure. Try to accurately capture the authentic tone as well as the content of your inner critic's voice.

Then write a response letter, appreciating the inner critic for its usefulness in your life, but also distinguishing which of its messages you choose to listen to, and those which are no longer useful. End by finding a way to make peace with your inner critic, acknowledging your continuing, maturing relationship.

Notes and ideas:

Prep Stairway before ANY Smart Storytelling Opportunity

Your Step-by-step guide to using smart storytelling to build trust and having the freedom to be the person you know you are.

1. **Clarify 'your brief.'**

    Be sure to know what is expected of you. Make sure you know what they are asking you to talk about. Or make sure you know what the meeting needs to be about. Ensure you know the time limits you have. If it's a more formal speaking opportunity, get clear on what equipment will be there. Do they want an inspirational talk, a workshop, or a seminar?

2. **Mark out time in your diary to prepare**. Schedule time in your diary. At least an hour.

3. **Identify your intent and CTA.**

    Use the spider diagram approach. Remember, intent is all about you and CTA is what you want them to do for you.

4. **Identify your core messages.**

    Make sure they *fit your brief*. Then go back over your River of Life (if needs be) or look through your Bank of Stories and identify relevant stories that get your message across.

5. **Identify any relevant storytelling techniques** you wish to deploy.

    Remember RELEVANCY: to you, to your intent, to your CTA, to your stories and core messages, and relevance to your audience as well as relevance to the situation you are speaking in.

6. **Practise, practice, practice.** Practice out loud.

    Review what you've done. Perhaps let it settle for a couple of days (if you have time). Come back to it and make revisions. Practice out loud until you feel you own it. Practice with any relevant equipment you'll be using. Remember, never practice learning 'it' like a script. Practice it so it feels part of you.

7. Enjoy yourself. Have fun. It's you are a smart storyteller.

Notes and ideas:

A final word then

The truth of this life is to know yourself, trust yourself and be yourself; only then will you be truly trustworthy.

I've run far enough away from happiness. Far away from me. I no longer run away. I have run enough with one-eye searching for the love of others, searching for appreciation, acceptance, and fitting in. I don't anymore. I live as me. I live with intent in every situation, knowing how each moment fits neatly into my life's purpose. Winning back the trust of myself and others.

Designing the content of this book, living by its practices, and helping others to do the same has given me that purpose. With doubt and belief running alongside me and coursing through me like a raging torrent, I help successful people create new memories that pave the way for them to be excellent – letting go of the thoughts and feelings that serve them no longer. That is Smart Storytelling. There's no real secret to cultivating an attitude of steady thinking and feeling. There is no holy grail to standing in your power and using your stories to connect and engage. There is a dedicated practice required to build the self-belief needed in Smart Storytelling. One such practice is smart storytelling.

The joy of this life is singing our song in the chorus of life. The pages of this book will help you do just this. Do it now.

Notes and ideas:

Printed in Great Britain
by Amazon